THE LIFE OF JESUS

Nihil Obstat: Right Reverend Archimandrite Francis Vivona, S.T.M., J.C.L.
Imprimatur: Most Reverend Joseph A. Pepe, D.D., J.C.D.
Date: August 12, 2014

By Bart Tesoriero
Illustrated by Miguel D. Lopez

ISBN 978-1-61796-141-0
© Copyright 2014 by Aquinas Kids, Phoenix, Arizona
Printed in China

The Birth of Jesus

A lovely young lady named Mary lived in Nazareth. She was engaged to Joseph, a strong and quiet carpenter, whose ancestor was King David, the most famous king of Israel.

God sent the angel Gabriel to Mary, to ask if she would become the mother of His Son. Mary asked, "How can this be, since I am a virgin?" The angel replied, "The Holy Spirit will come upon you, and the power of the Most High will overshadow you. Therefore the child to be born will be called holy, the Son of God." Mary answered, "Let it be done unto me according to your word." Soon afterwards, an angel visited Joseph in a dream, and told him to be not afraid to take Mary as his wife.

The Roman ruler had ordered everyone to be enrolled in the town of their ancestors. Joseph and Mary journeyed to Bethlehem, where Joseph found a little stable. That night, Mary gave birth to her son, Jesus. She wrapped Him in warm clothing and laid Him in a manger. The angel of the Lord appeared to nearby shepherds, saying, "Do not be afraid! Behold, I bring you good news of great joy: Today in the city of David a savior is born for you who is Messiah and Lord. Glory to God in the highest, and on earth peace to men of good will!"

The Presentation in the Temple

Forty days after Jesus was born, Joseph and Mary took Him to the temple in Jerusalem to present Him to the Lord. Now in Jerusalem there lived an old man named Simeon.

Simeon was very good and he loved God very much. The Holy Spirit had told Simeon that he would not die until he had seen the Messiah of the Lord, the promised Redeemer.

On this day, then, the Spirit prompted Simeon to come into the Temple, where he saw Joseph, Mary, and Jesus. Simeon took the child into his arms, and he blessed God. Simeon said, "Now, Master, You may let Your servant go in peace, according to Your word, for my eyes have seen Your salvation, which you prepared in sight of all the peoples, a light for revelation to the Gentiles, and glory for Your people Israel."

Simeon blessed Mary and Joseph. Then he turned to Mary and said, "This child is destined for the fall and rise of many in Israel. He shall be a sign that will be contradicted. A sword shall also pierce your own soul, so that the thoughts of many hearts may be revealed."

The Boy Jesus

Joseph and Mary returned to Bethlehem. One night, while Joseph was sleeping, an angel appeared to him in a dream. "Get up Joseph!" the angel said. "Take the child and His mother and flee to Egypt, because King Herod is searching for the child to kill Him!"

Joseph took Mary and Jesus that very night into Egypt. After a time, Herod died, and the angel told Joseph, "Rise, take the child and His mother and return to Israel, for those who sought the child's life are dead." Joseph took his little family back to Nazareth, and there Jesus grew up.

The town of Nazareth was hilly, and one hill was quite high. Jesus might have climbed that very hill as a boy. On a clear day, He could see Mount Carmel, where Elijah the prophet had called down fire from heaven. From the hilltop, Jesus could also glimpse the Sea of Galilee, with its shimmering blue water reflecting sparkles from the sun. Like all children, Jesus probably liked feeling the warmth of the sun and the cool breezes caress His face.

It may have been in quiet places like this that Jesus spent time praying to "Abba," His heavenly Father. As Jesus grew in size, He also grew in His heart, closer each day to those He loved, and to those who loved Him.

The Home at Nazareth

Like other homes in Nazareth, the home of Joseph and Mary may have contained a few rooms joined to a courtyard shared by other families. Mary cooked and served in one room, leaving the other rooms for sleeping and storage. Joseph used one room for his workshop where he could also keep his tools.

Joseph worked hard building and repairing homes, and making plows, tables, and other items. Mary prepared meals, cleaned, sewed clothes, tended the garden, and took good care of her husband and son. She prepared dinners of vegetable soup or stew, with figs, grapes, or apples for dessert. Mary also churned goats' milk into buttermilk, yogurt, and cheese.

Jesus learned to read, write, and to work a trade. Every Saturday, the family celebrated the Sabbath, a day set aside for the worship of the God of Israel and for a rest. Mary gathered the family around her and lit the Sabbath candles. Joseph intoned the Sabbath prayers.

In Nazareth, Jesus came to know rich people and poor people, good people and bad people. He also learned to hear the voice of His heavenly Father. His time was approaching.

The Finding in the Temple

Every year Joseph and Mary took Jesus with them
to Jerusalem for the feast of Passover, as God had
commanded the Jews when He delivered them from
Egypt. When Jesus was twelve years old, He went with
His parents as usual. Afterwards, they returned home,
but Jesus remained behind without their knowing it.

Joseph and Mary thought that Jesus was traveling with
His cousins and relatives. When they realized that He
was missing, they returned to Jerusalem to look for
Him. After three days they finally found Jesus in the
temple, sitting with the teachers and priests, listening to
them and asking them questions. Everyone who heard
Jesus was amazed at His understanding and His answers.

Mary said, "Son, why have You done this to us? Your
father and I have looked for You with sorrow!" Jesus
answered, "Did you not know I must be in my Father's
house?" Mary and Joseph did not understand His answer.

Then Jesus returned to Nazareth with His parents, and
He obeyed them in all things. Mary kept all these words
in her heart. She thought about them many times.
Meanwhile, Jesus grew in wisdom, age, and favor before
God and all the people.

12

The Baptism of Jesus

When Jesus was 30 years old, He left His home in Nazareth. He came to the Jordan River, to be baptized by His cousin John. John the Baptist lived in the desert, where he spent much time in prayer. John wore a garment of camel's skin, and ate only grasshoppers and wild honey.

John was baptizing the people in the river Jordan for the forgiveness of sins. When he saw Jesus, John was unwilling to baptize Him, for he knew He was holy. But Jesus told John to do so, because that was what God wanted.

After Jesus was baptized, suddenly the sky opened up, and John saw the Holy Spirit, in the shape of a dove, come down from heaven and rest upon Jesus. The people around heard a voice from heaven, which said, "This is my Beloved Son, in whom I am well pleased."

John said, "Behold the Lamb of God, who takes away the sin of the world. The One who sent me to baptize told me, 'When you see the Holy Spirit descend like a dove on someone, it is he who will baptize with the Holy Spirit.' Now I have seen and testify that Jesus is the Son of God."

Jesus Heals a Blind Man

One day, Jesus and His disciples came to the town of Jericho. A blind man named Bartimaeus sat by the road, begging. He asked someone what was happening. "Jesus is passing by!" they told him. Bartimaeus cried out, "Jesus, Son of David, have pity on me!" "Be quiet!" the people told him. "You are making too much noise!" But Bartimaeus only cried out louder, "Jesus, Son of David, have pity on me!"

Jesus stopped. "Call the man," He said. The friends of Bartimaeus ran over to him. "Quick!" they said, "Get up! Jesus is calling for you!"

Jesus looked at Bartimaeus with love and asked him, "What do you want me to do for you?" Bartimaeus said, "Master, I want to see." Jesus smiled and said, "Go your way, my friend. Your faith has saved you."

Immediately the eyes of Bartimaeus were opened, and he was able to see. He rejoiced and shouted, "I can see! I can see!" Then he followed Jesus on the way.

The Sermon on the Mount

One day Jesus went up on a mountain to teach His disciples about God. He said to them, "Blessed are those who are poor, who trust in God, for the kingdom of heaven belongs to them."

Jesus continued, "Blessed are those who feel sad, for God will comfort them. Blessed are those who are quiet and humble, for the earth will be given to them. Blessed are those who want to be good, for they shall be satisfied. Blessed are those who help others with mercy, for mercy shall be given to them."

Jesus looked at His followers with love, and He said, "Blessed are the pure of heart, for they will see God. Blessed are those who make peace, for they shall be called the children of God. Blessed are those who suffer for doing what is right, for the kingdom of heaven is theirs."

Jesus taught His listeners many things that day. "Seek God first," He said, "and everything else will be given to you." As He spoke, the gentle winds blew and the little red flowers danced in the breeze.

"Remember to forgive others," Jesus told His followers. "If you forgive others, your heavenly Father will also forgive you."

Jesus and the Children

Little children loved to be around Jesus because they knew that He loved them. His warm smile and big hugs made them feel good. And Jesus loved the little children. He liked telling them stories about farmers and fishermen, shepherds and kings. He would listen to them, and they would listen to Him.

One day some mothers and fathers brought their children to Jesus. They wanted Jesus to lay His hands on the children and bless them. The apostles cried, "Stop! Jesus is too busy to see your children!" But Jesus said, "Let the children come to me, and do not stop them. My kingdom belongs to such as these. Unless you become like little children, you shall not enter the kingdom of God."

Then all the children ran up to Jesus. They laughed as He smiled at them, hugged them, and blessed them. Jesus told them a story. Then He gave them back to their parents. When the children grew up, they remembered the Wonderful Storyteller who had loved them so much, and they followed Him.

The Miracle of the Loaves and Fishes

As Jesus walked the land, preaching about His Father in heaven, news of Him began to spread. People heard of His miracles and the many wonderful things He was doing, and they wanted to learn more. They traveled a long way to see and hear Jesus.

One time many, many people gathered around Jesus in a distant place, far from any towns. They were so fascinated they missed lunch and dinner. More than 5,000 people had been with Jesus all day long, and they were getting hungry.

The apostles told Jesus, "Send the people out to buy food." Jesus answered, "Give them food yourselves." The disciples replied, "There is a boy here who has five barley loaves and two fish; but what good are these for so many?"

Jesus said, "Have the people sit down." Then He took the loaves and the fish, blessed them, and gave them to His disciples to give to the people. Everyone ate their fill, and the disciples collected twelve baskets of leftovers!

Just as Jesus had promised, God provides what we need, and more, when we put our trust in Him.

The Good Shepherd

Jesus had come to earth to tell people about God. He came to help us get to know God as our Father, as Someone who really cares for us and loves us so much! Jesus told stories to help people understand God better.

"Once upon a time," Jesus said, "there was a shepherd who had many sheep. Even though he had a lot of sheep, he knew each of them by name. Every day he took them out into the fields and meadows so they could eat good rich grass and drink cool water. They liked their shepherd.

"One day, a little lamb wandered away from the flock and got lost. When the shepherd realized his lamb was missing, he left his other sheep and went to find it. He looked up in the mountains and down by the streams. Finally he found the frightened little lamb, put it on his shoulders, and brought it home. The shepherd said, 'Rejoice with me, for I have found my sheep that was lost!'"

Jesus said, "I am the Good Shepherd. I know my sheep, and they know me. My sheep follow me. If they get lost, I search for them until I find them. I bring them back home with me. I care so much for my sheep that I will even lay down my life for them."

The Last Supper

Jesus spent three years preaching the Good News, teaching people, and healing the sick all over Israel. Then He and His disciples traveled to Jerusalem for the Passover, as they did every year. This time, Jesus rode into Jerusalem on a donkey. He was entering the city as a king of peace. A great crowd of people came out to meet Him, waving palm branches and crying, "Hosanna! Blessed is he who comes in the name of the Lord!"

Later that week, Jesus sat down with His apostles for the Passover meal. Judas left the meal early. He had decided to turn Jesus over to His enemies. During the meal, Jesus took the bread, blessed it, broke it, and gave it to His disciples saying, "Take and eat; this is my body." Then He took a chalice of wine, gave thanks, and passed it around. Jesus said, "Drink this, all of you, for this is my blood, to be poured out for the forgiveness of sins. Do this in memory of me."

Jesus and His disciples went out to the Garden of Gethsemane. Jesus became very troubled. "Father, if You are willing, You can take this suffering away from me; but may Your Will be done." Judas came into the garden with a crowd of soldiers and betrayed Jesus with a kiss. Then the soldiers arrested Jesus, and His friends ran away.

Jesus Carries the Cross

The soldiers put Jesus in a prison for the night. When morning came, the guards brought Jesus before the elders of the people, the chief priests, and the scribes. Many witnesses told false stories about Him. Jesus did not answer a word. Finally the high priest asked Him, "Are you the Messiah, the Son of God?" Jesus answered, "I am." They all cried, "He is worthy of death!"

The guards then led Jesus away to the Roman governor of Judea. His name was Pontius Pilate. Pilate asked Jesus if He was the king of the Jews. Pilate did not want to put Jesus to death. In order to satisfy the enemies of Jesus, Pilate ordered his soldiers to beat Jesus with whips. They put a crown of thorns on His head. Then Pilate brought Jesus out to the people. They all cried, "Crucify him! Crucify him!" And so, Pilate condemned Jesus to death.

The soldiers laid a heavy cross on Jesus' shoulders and made Him carry it up to the Mount of Calvary, where He was to be crucified. Many people shouted at Jesus and made fun of Him, but others felt very sad for Jesus.

As Jesus walked on the way, His mother Mary came to be with Him. She felt very sorrowful in her heart to see her son suffer. She knew that He loved us so much that He was willing to die for us.

Jesus Dies on the Cross

When they arrived at Calvary, the soldiers nailed
Jesus to the cross. Near the top of the cross,
Pilate had written the letters INRI. These letters
stood for the words, "Jesus of Nazareth, King of
the Jews." The soldiers hurt Jesus very much.
However, He looked up to heaven from the cross,
and prayed, "Father, forgive them, for they do not
know what they are doing."

Jesus saw His mother Mary standing at the foot of
the cross, with His beloved apostle, John. Jesus said
to His mother, "Woman, behold your son." Then
to John He said, "Behold your mother." And from
that hour John took Mary into his home.

Jesus then said, "I thirst!" A soldier dipped a
sponge into some common wine, and raised it to
Jesus. Jesus said, "It is finished. Father, into Your
hands I commit my spirit."

And bowing His head, Jesus died.

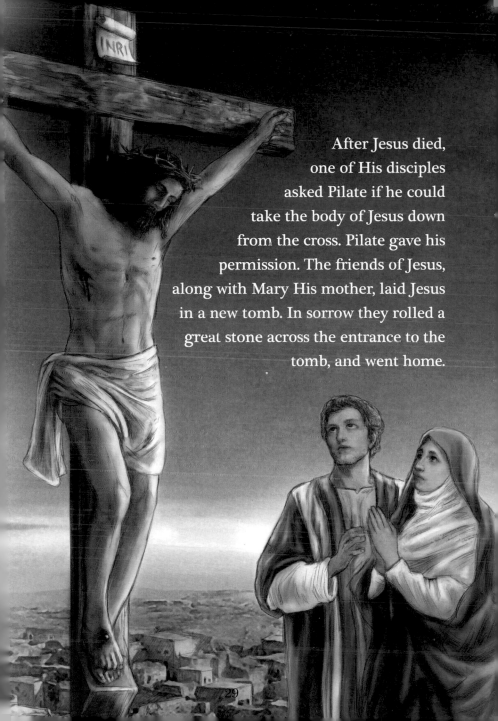

After Jesus died, one of His disciples asked Pilate if he could take the body of Jesus down from the cross. Pilate gave his permission. The friends of Jesus, along with Mary His mother, laid Jesus in a new tomb. In sorrow they rolled a great stone across the entrance to the tomb, and went home.

Jesus Rises from the Dead!

Very early in the morning on the first day of the week, the soldiers guarding the tomb felt the ground shake beneath their feet. In the middle of the earthquake, an angel of the Lord came down from heaven, rolled away the stone from the tomb, and sat upon it. He looked like lightening. His clothing was white as snow. The guards fell down in fear.

Suddenly, in a burst of great light, Jesus arose from the dead! He shined brighter than the sun. The soldiers cried out and ran away.

Just after sunrise, Mary Magdalene and some women came to the tomb to anoint the body of Jesus. "The stone is rolled away!" they cried. "Where is Jesus?" The angel said to them, "Do not be afraid! He is not here, for He is risen, just as He said. Come and see the place where He lay."

The women left the tomb quickly. They were very excited, and they ran to tell the good news to Peter and the other disciples. While they were on their way, Jesus Himself greeted them! The women bowed down to worship Him. Jesus said to them, "Do not be afraid. Go tell My brothers to go to Galilee, and there they will see Me."

Jesus Is with Us Always

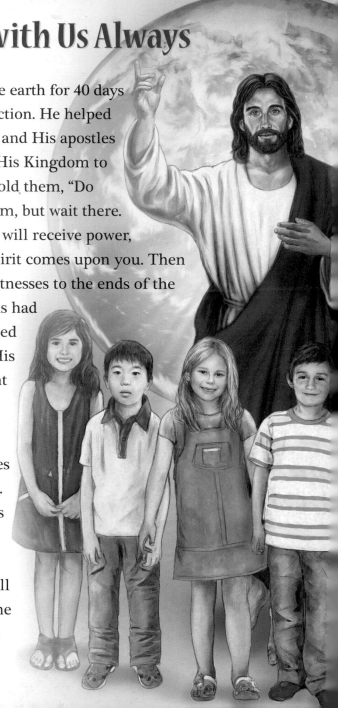

Jesus stayed on the earth for 40 days
after His Resurrection. He helped
His Mother Mary and His apostles
prepare to bring His Kingdom to
all people. Jesus told them, "Do
not leave Jerusalem, but wait there.
In a few days you will receive power,
when the Holy Spirit comes upon you. Then
you will be My witnesses to the ends of the
earth." When Jesus had
said this, He blessed
His Mother and His
disciples, and went
up into heaven.

Through our
Baptism, Jesus lives
now in our hearts.
His Spirit helps us
to love and obey
God our Father.
Someday Jesus will
return, to bring the
Kingdom forever.
Alleluia!